I0480695

This Book Belongs To

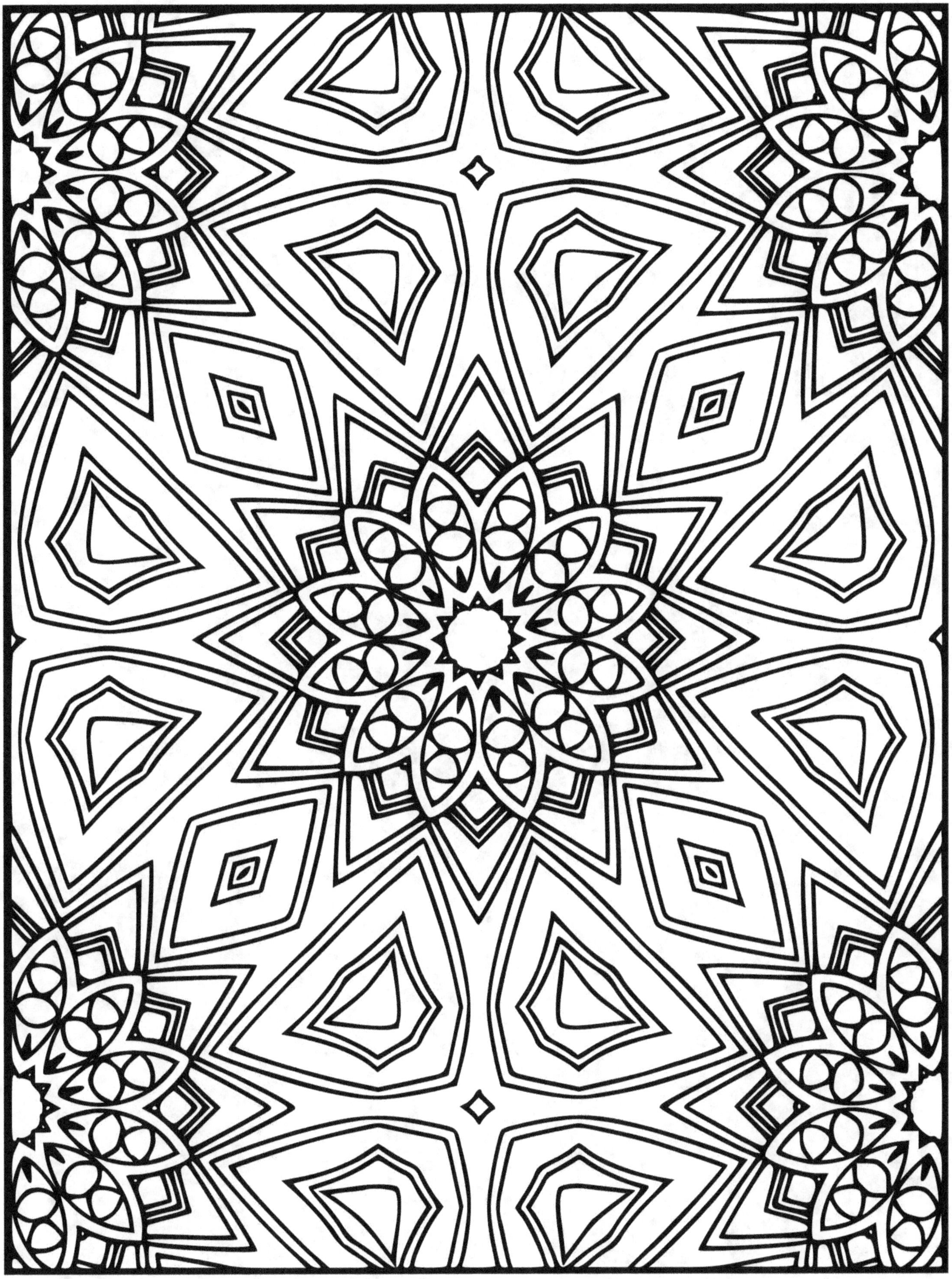

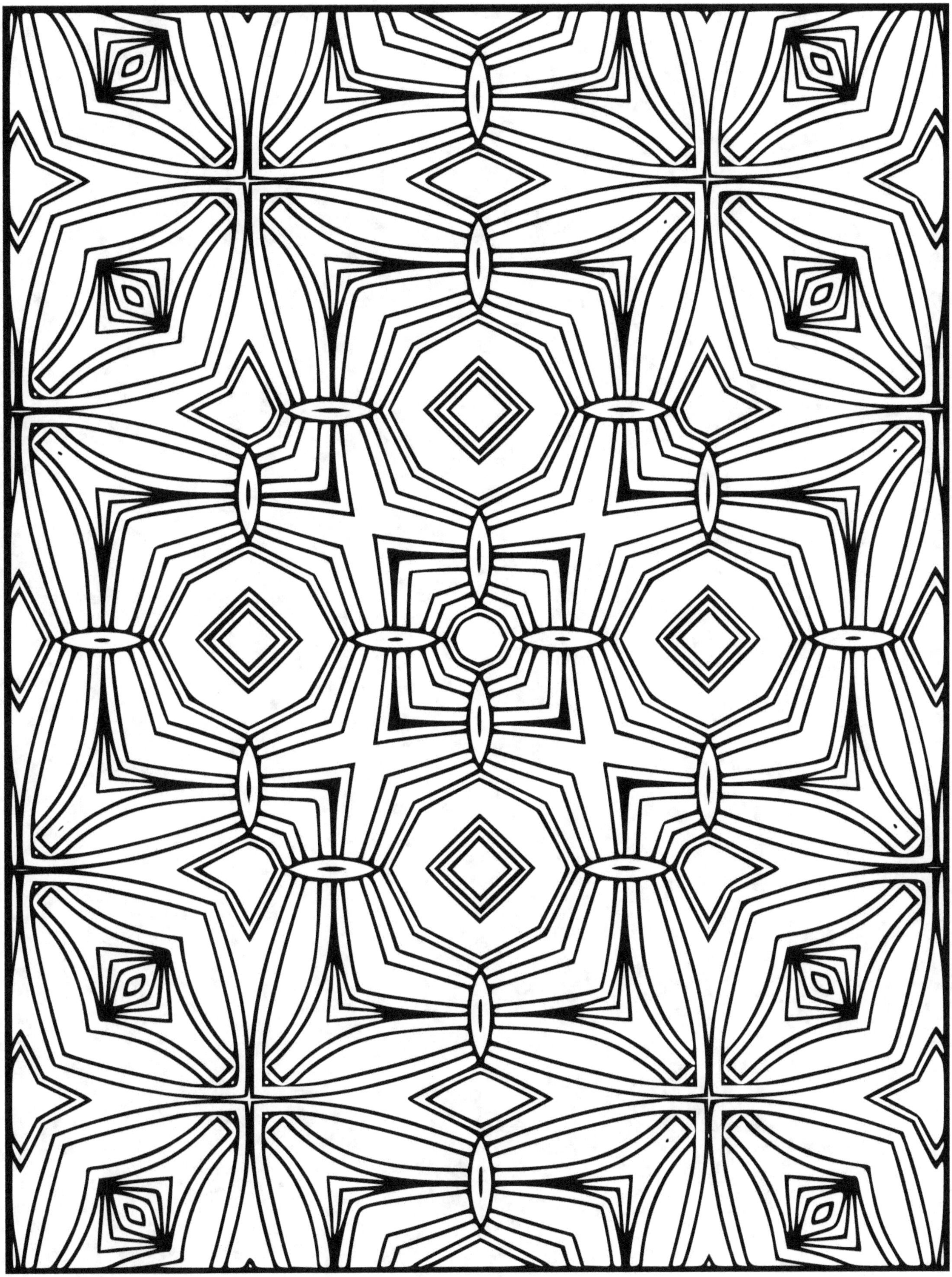

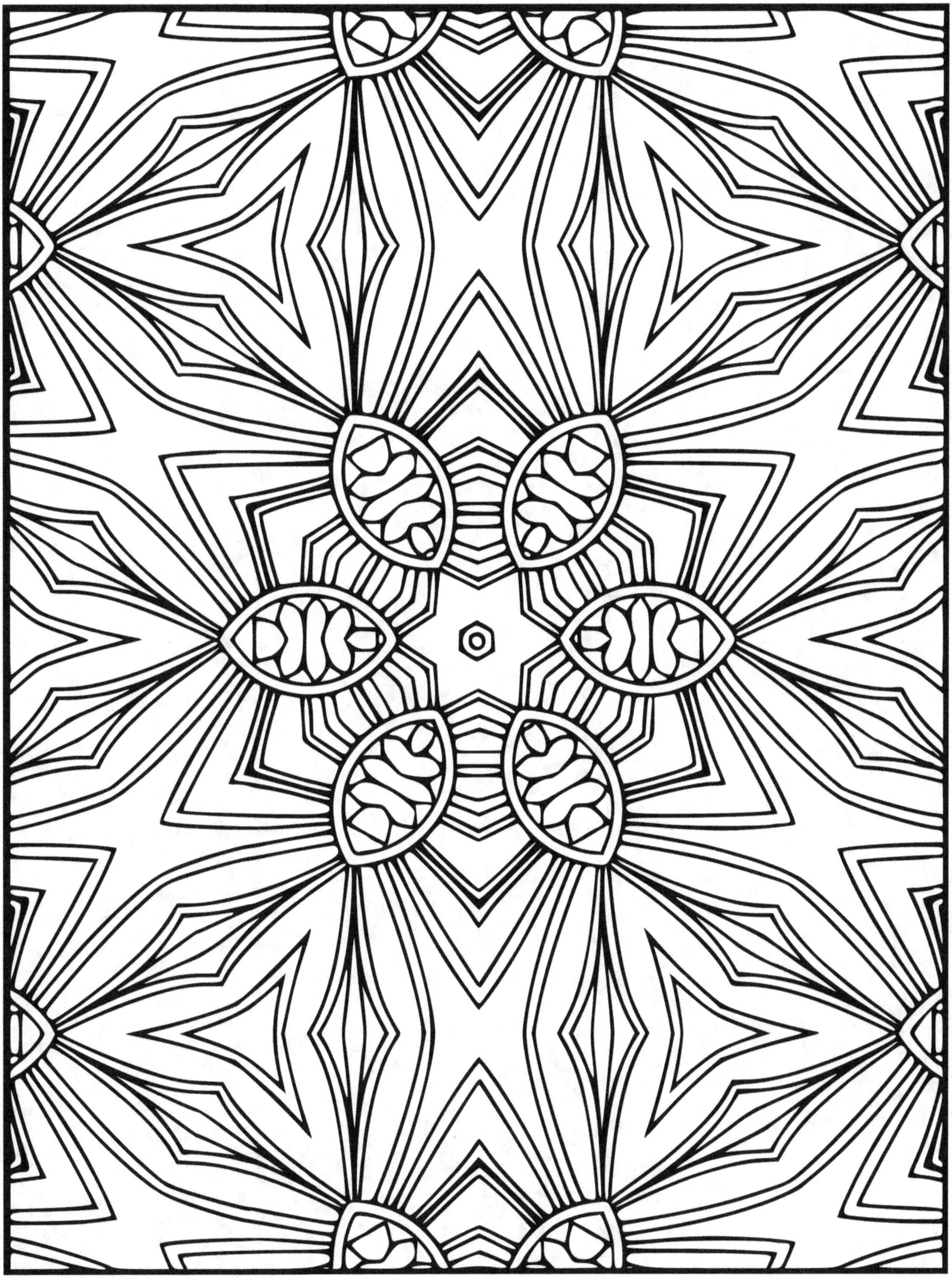

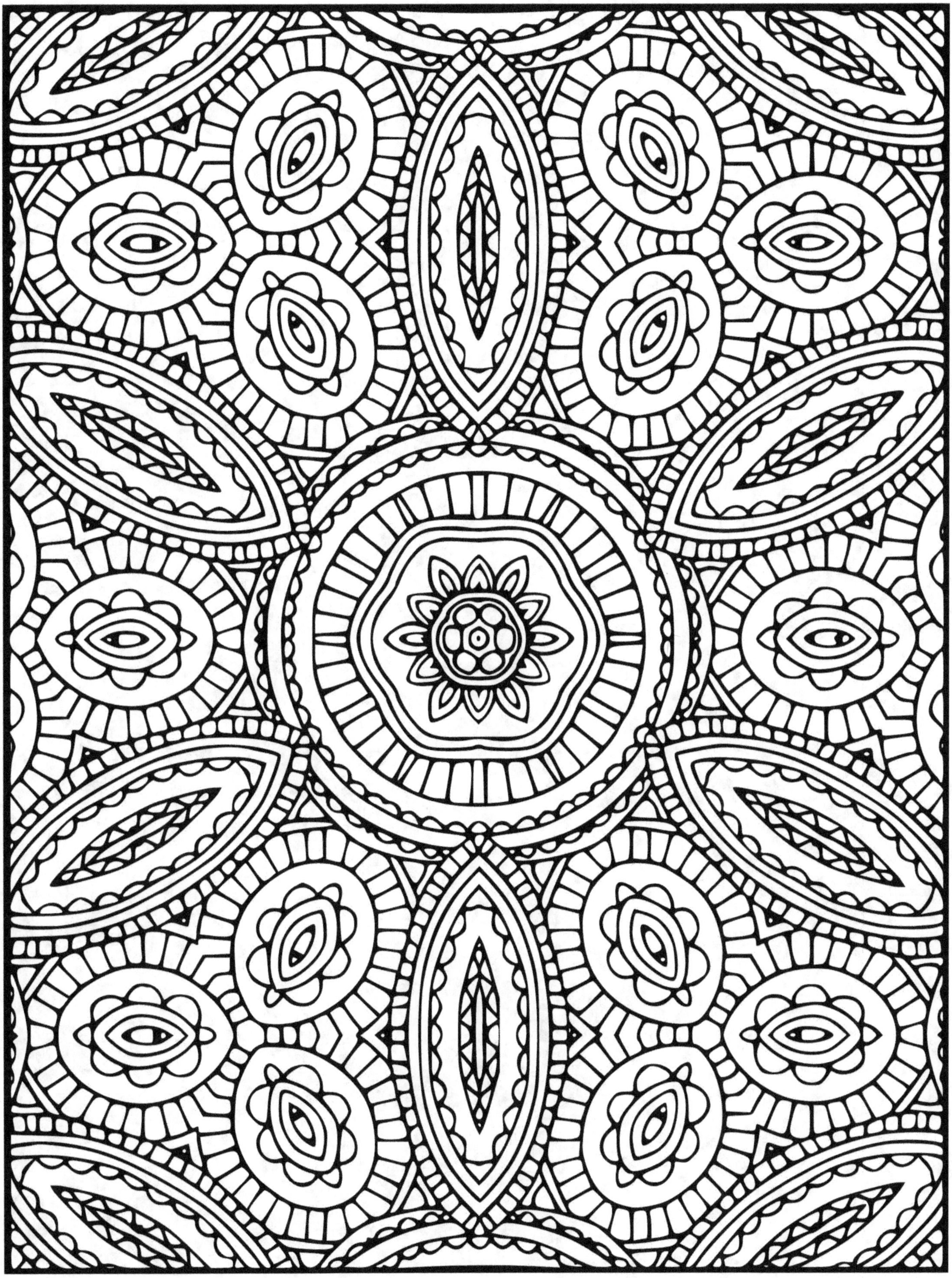

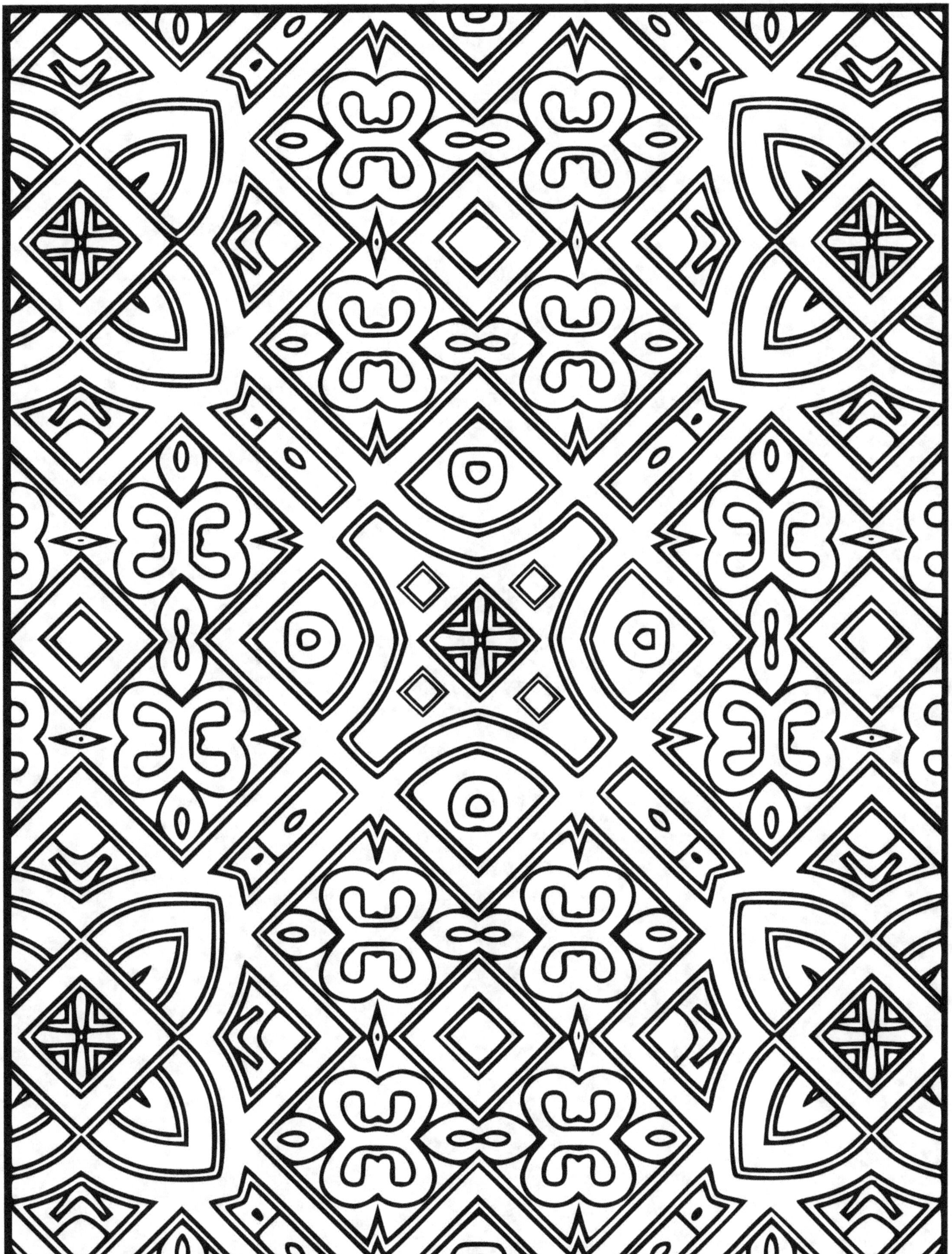

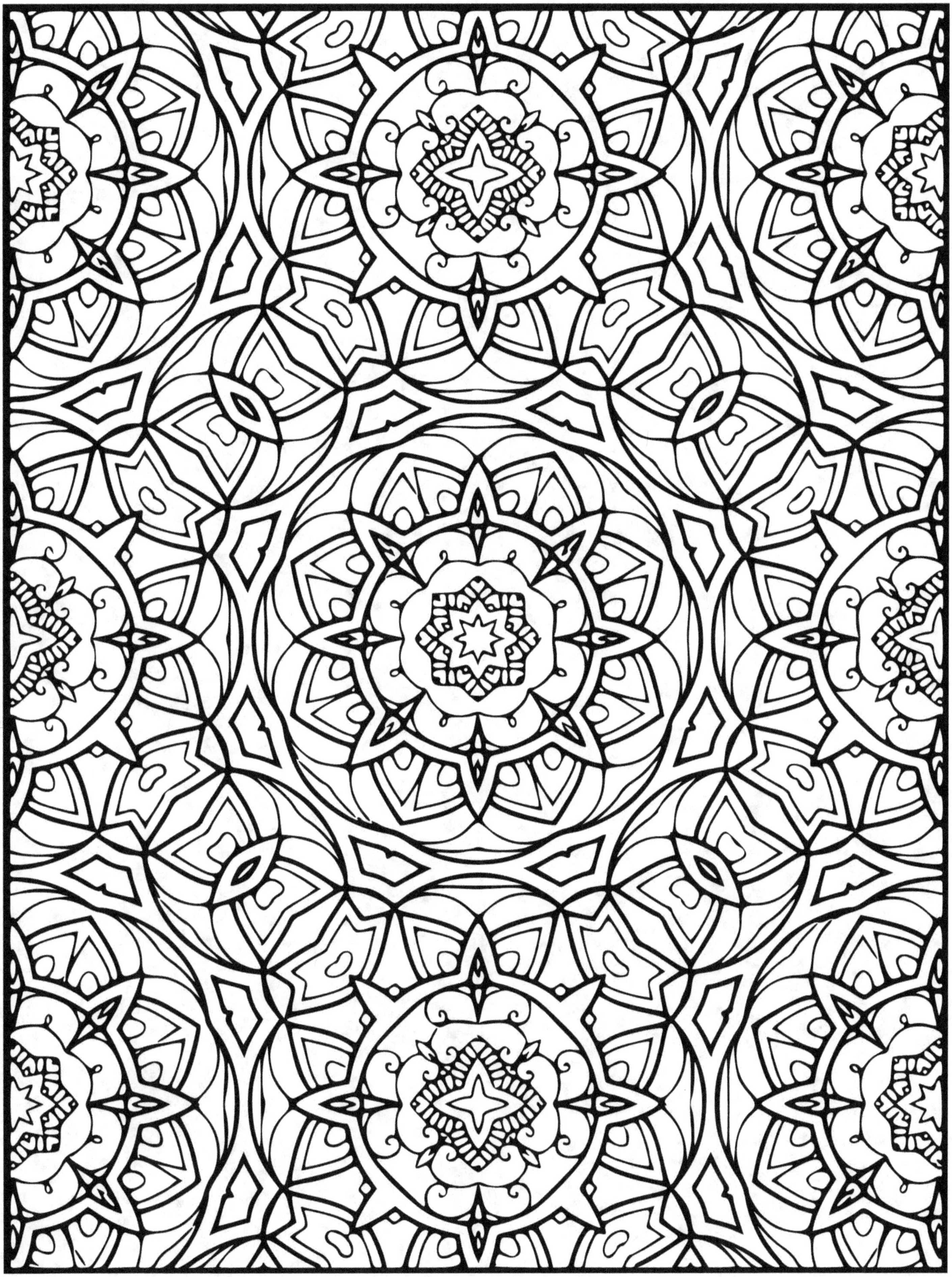

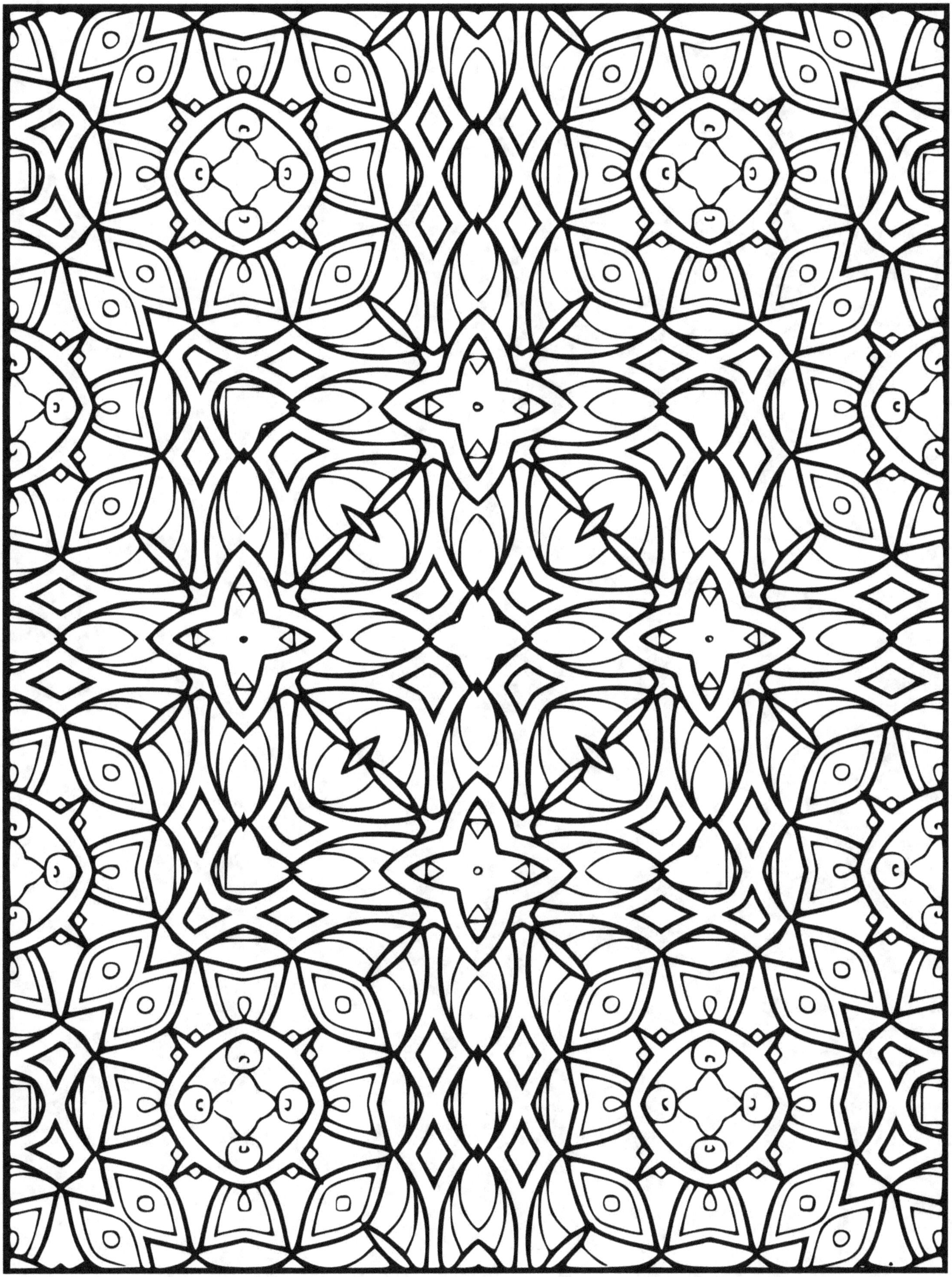

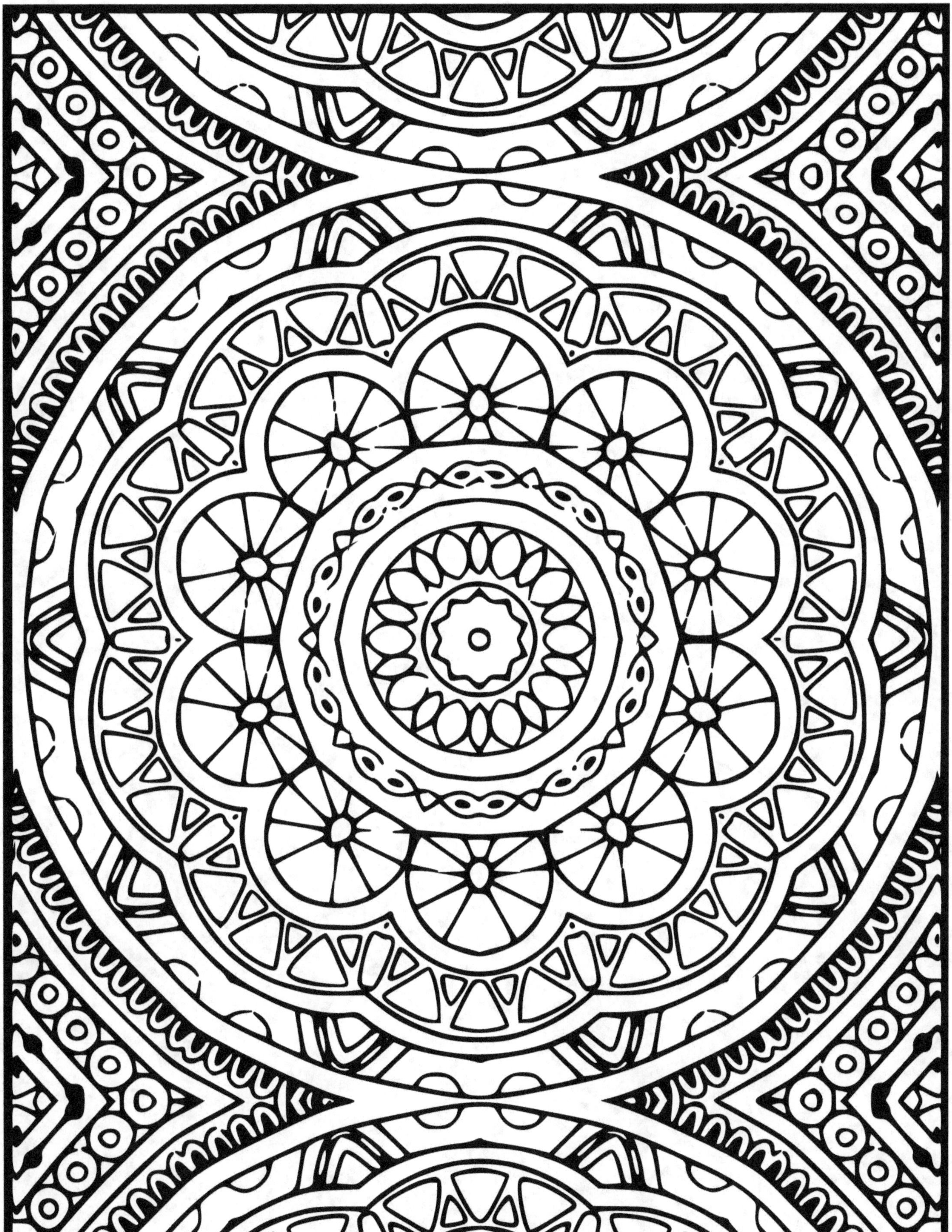

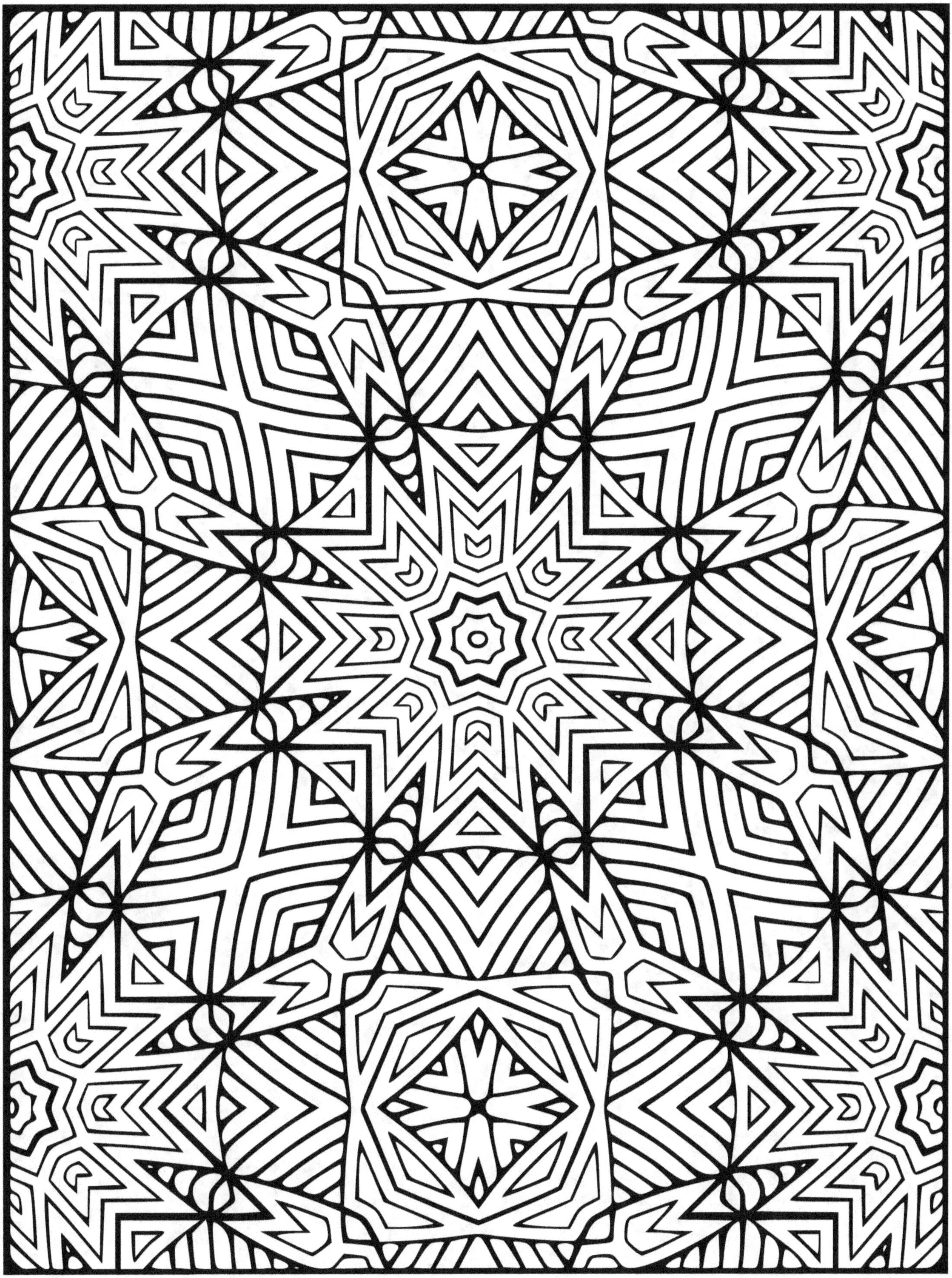

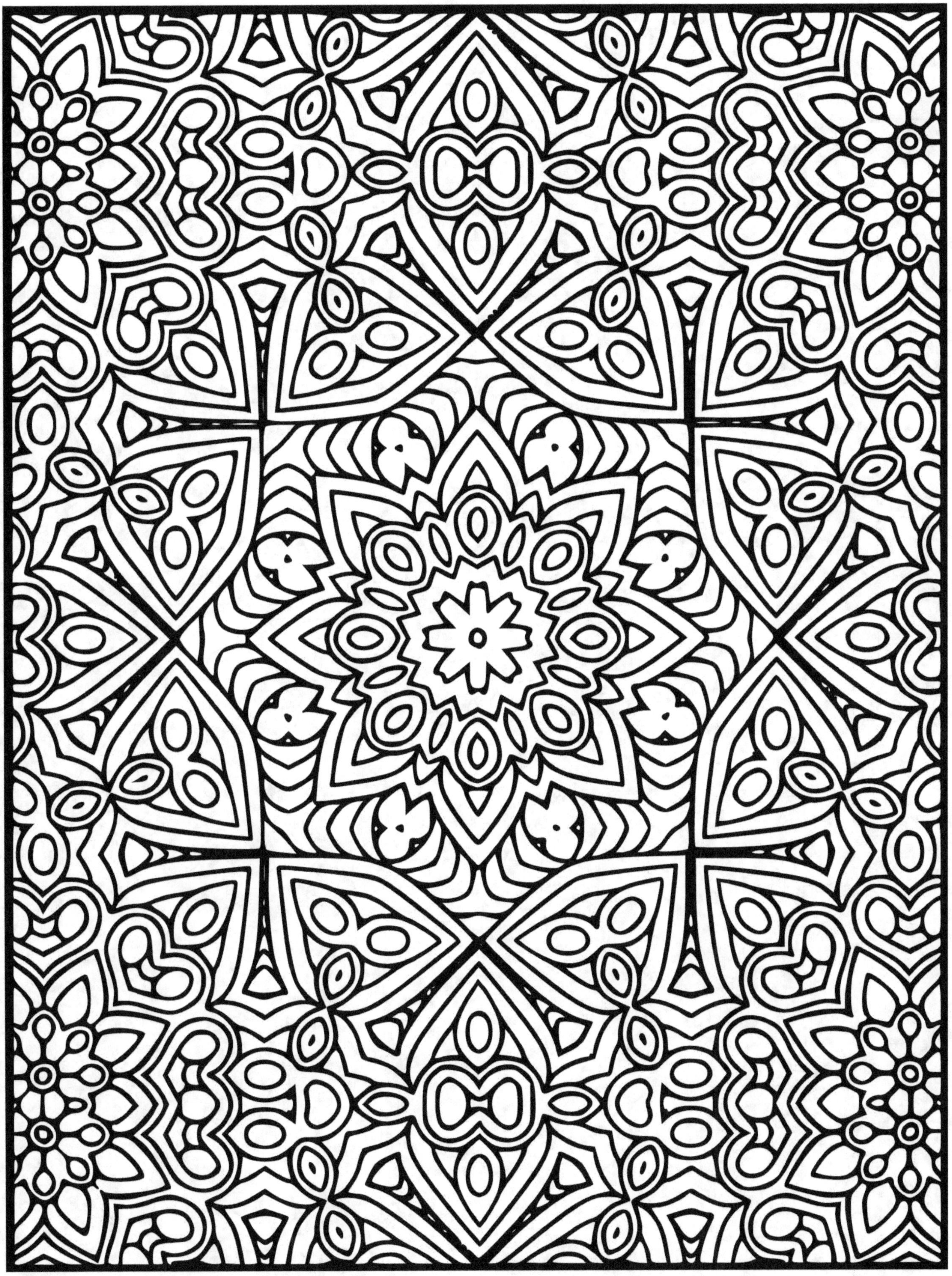

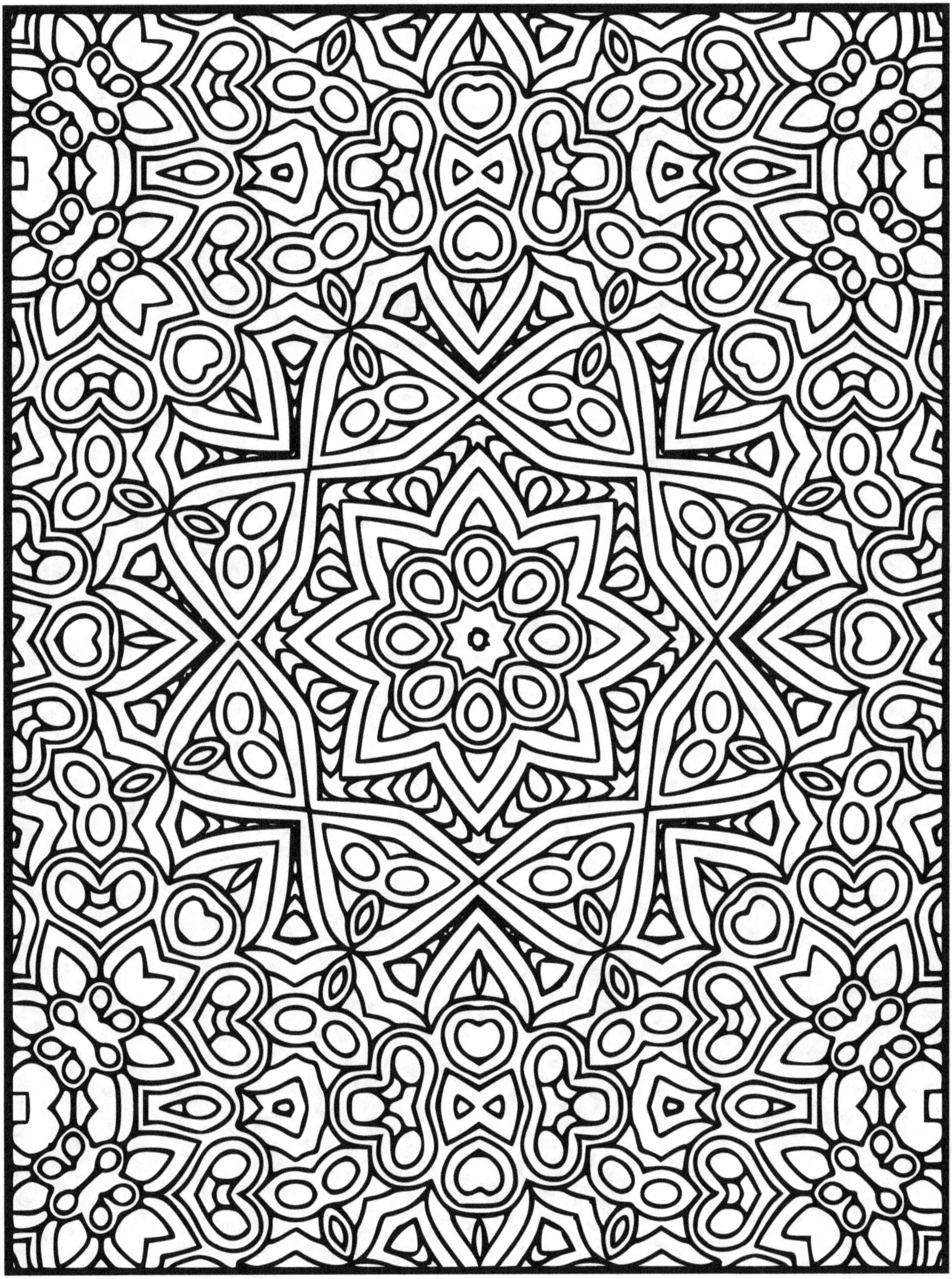

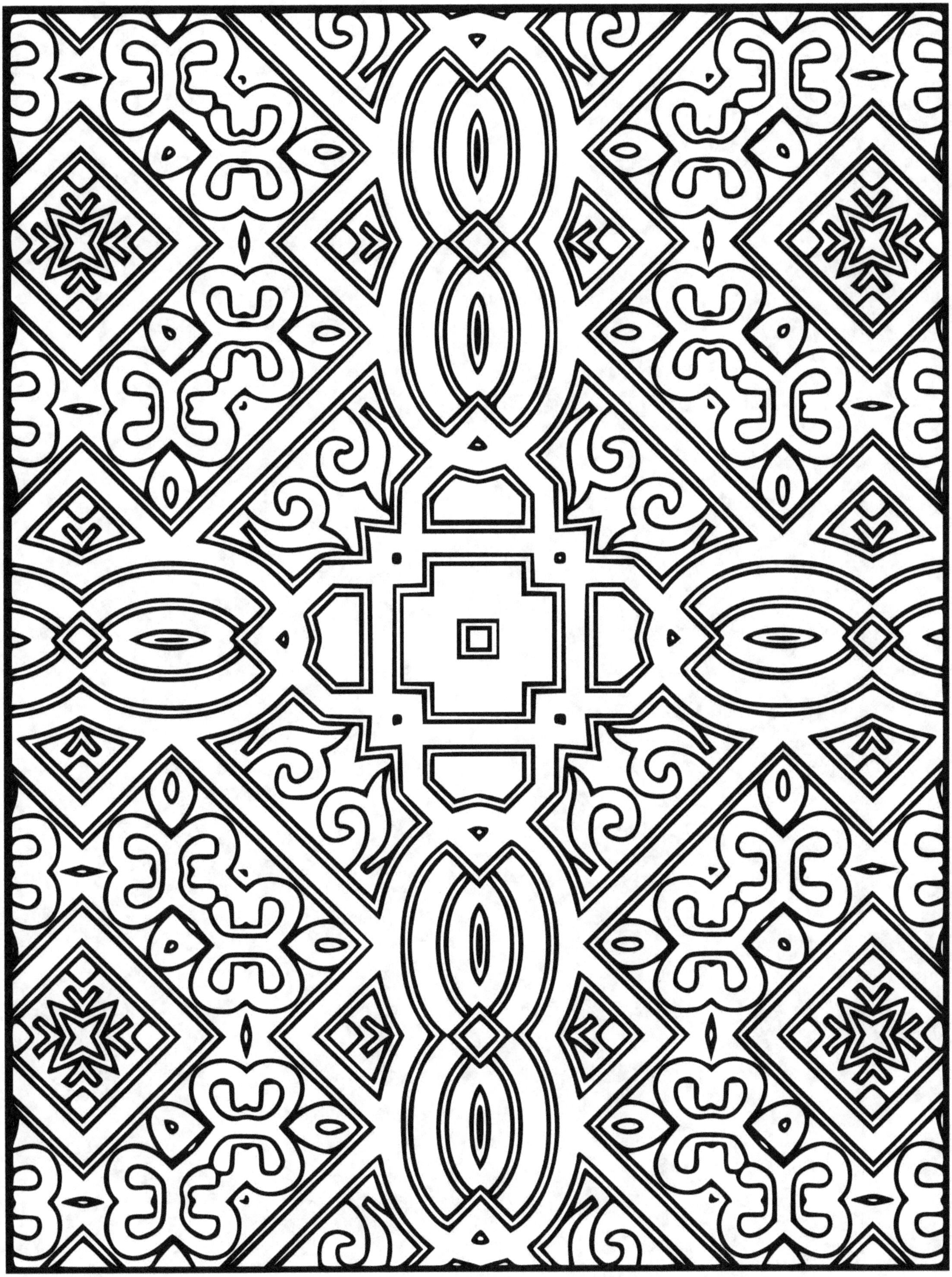

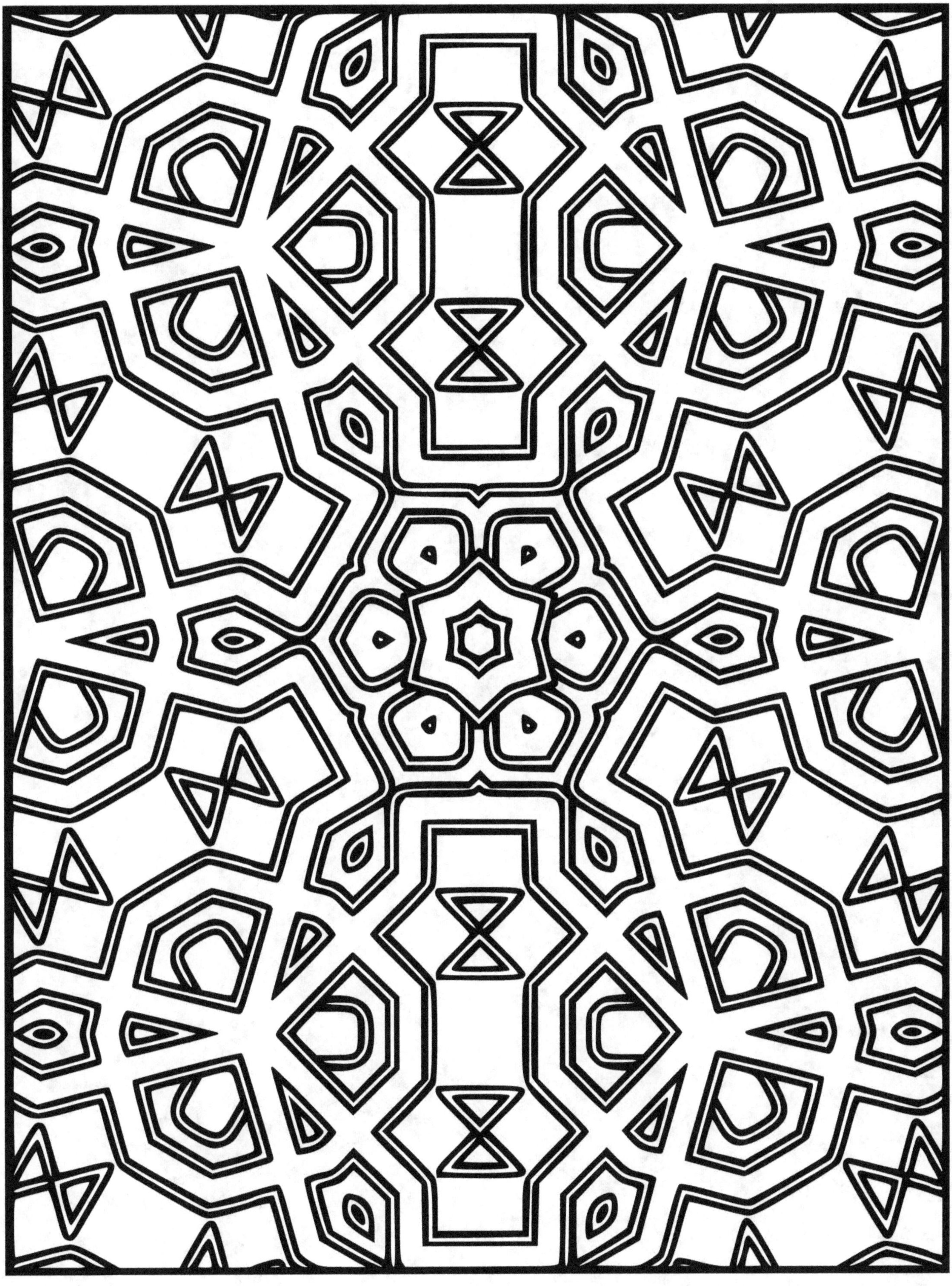

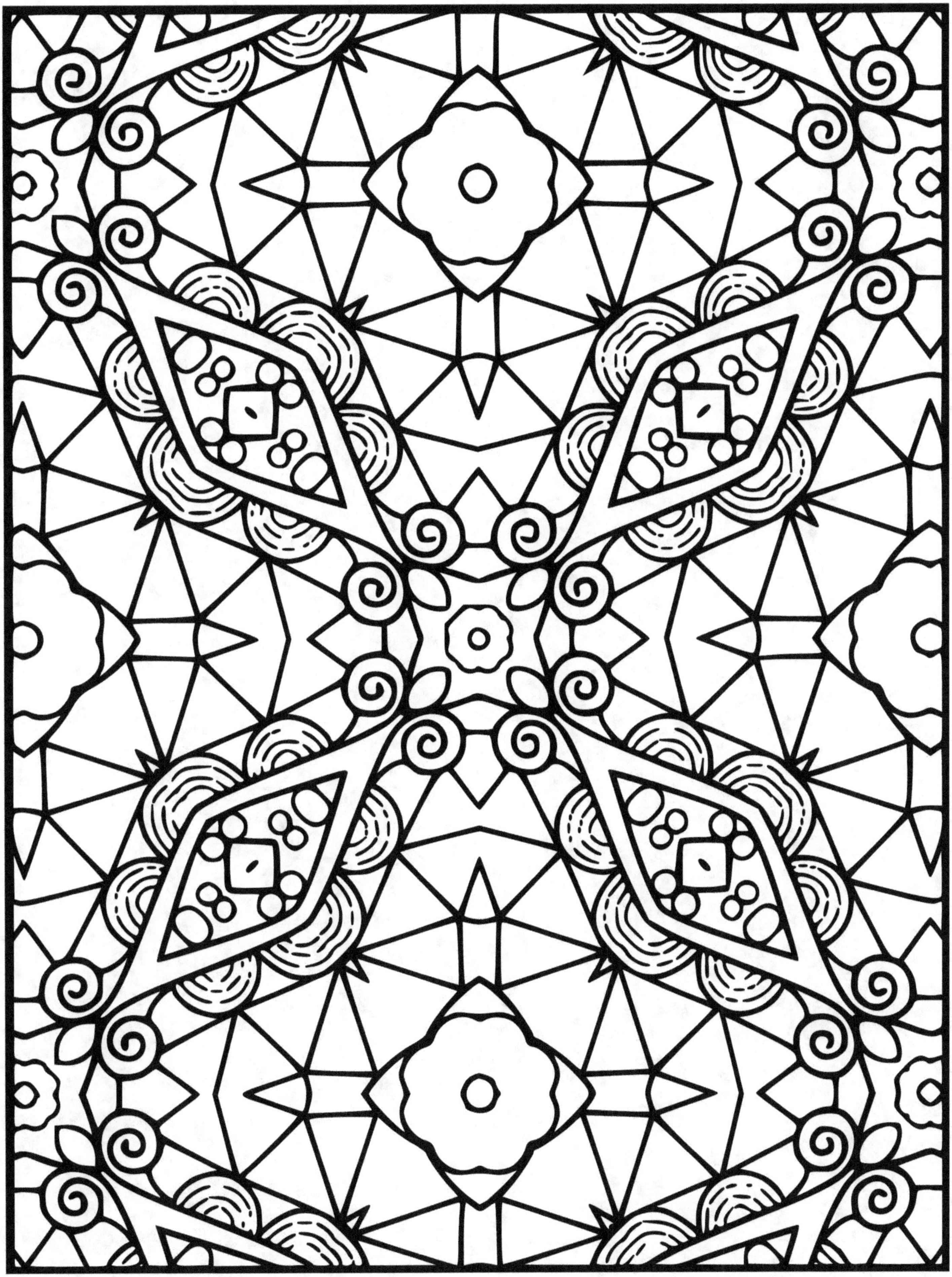

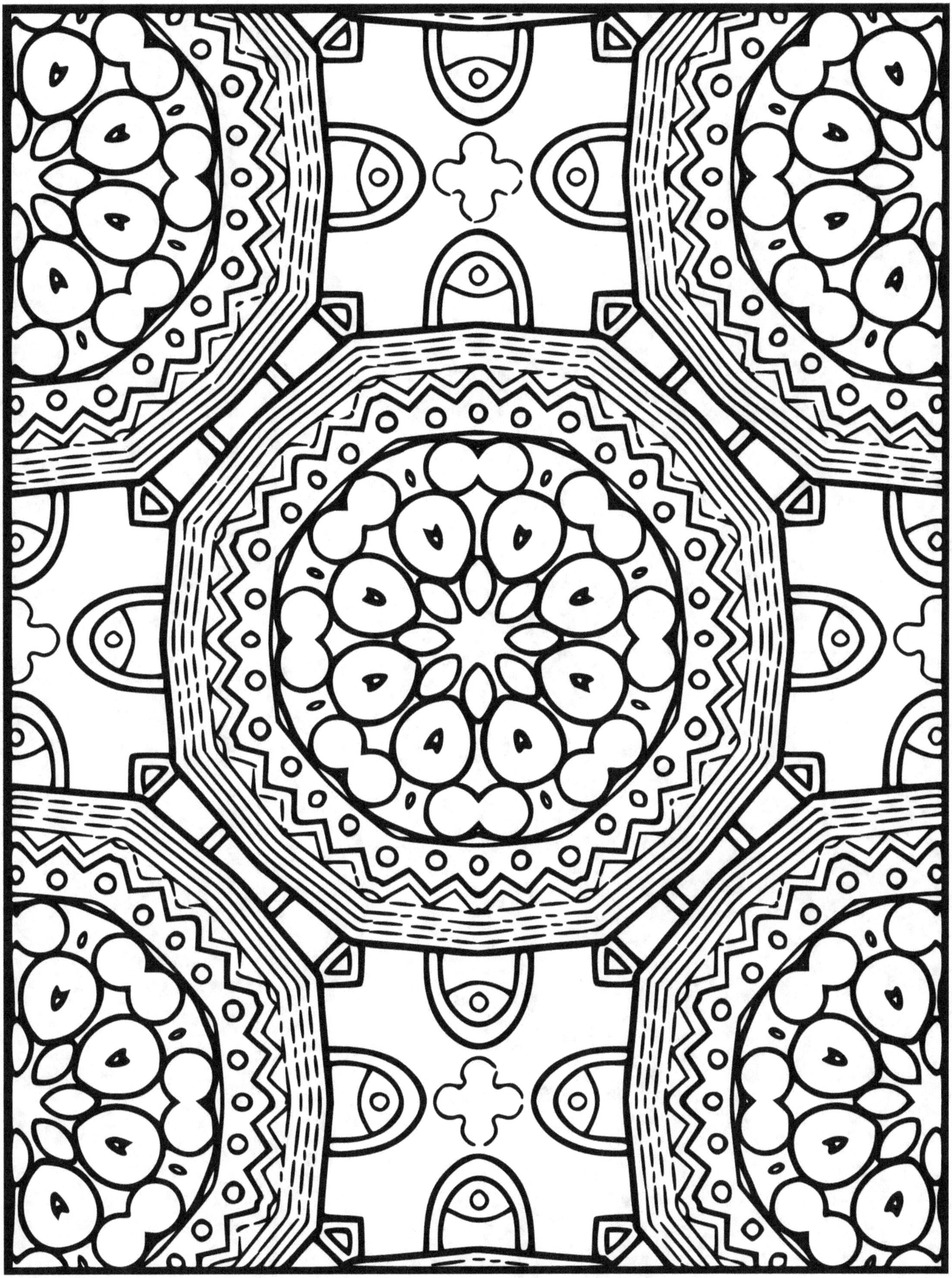

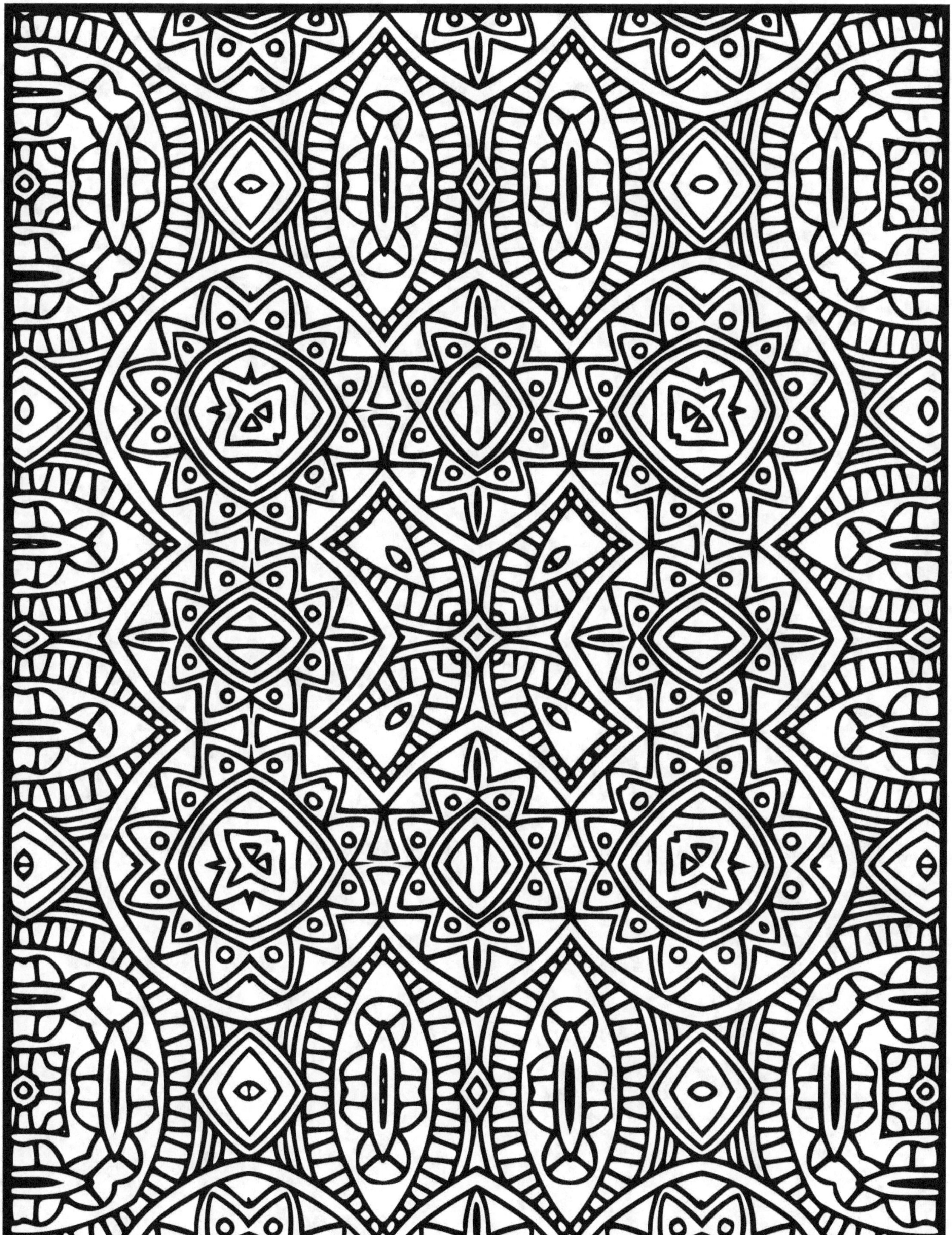

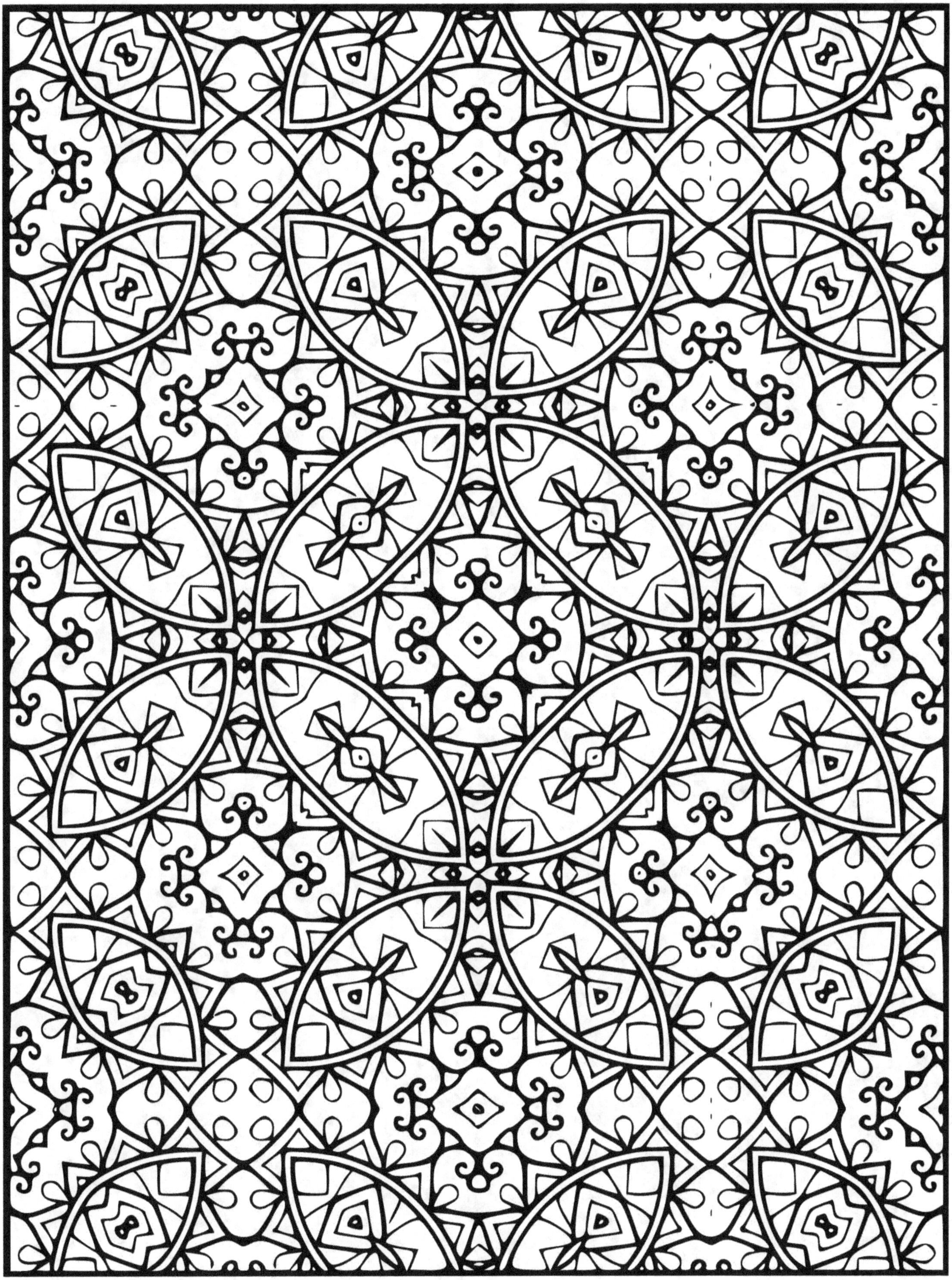

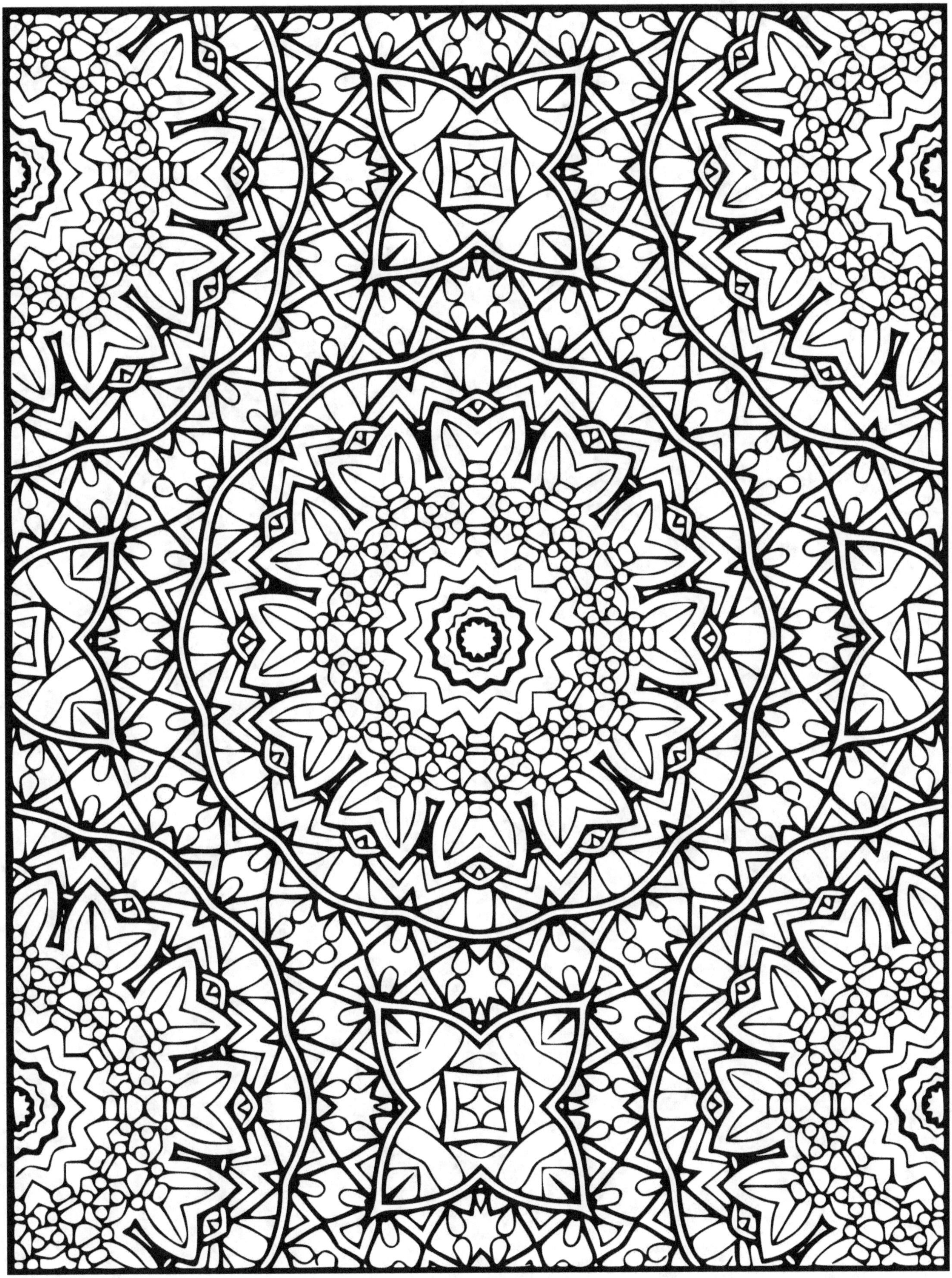

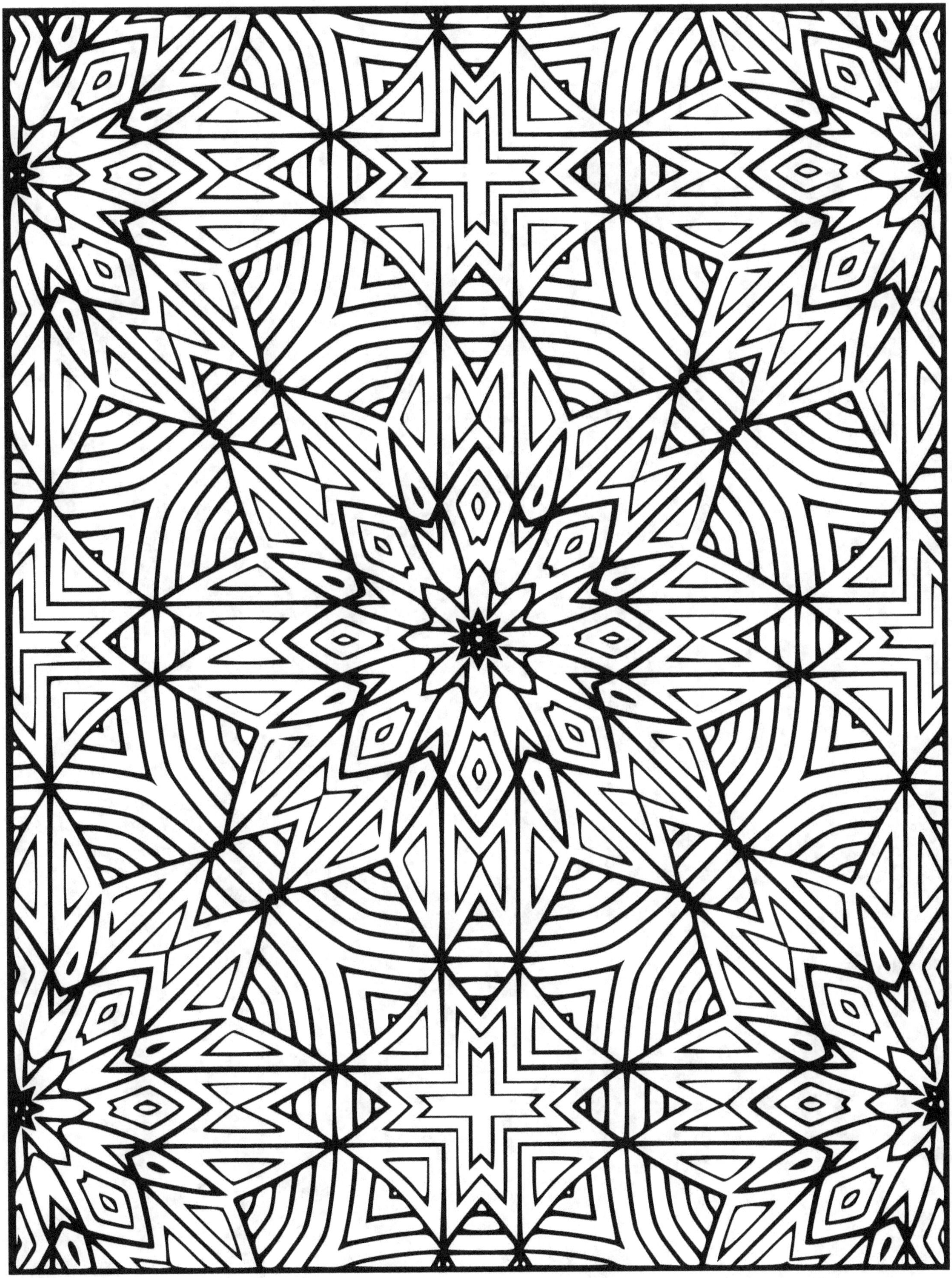

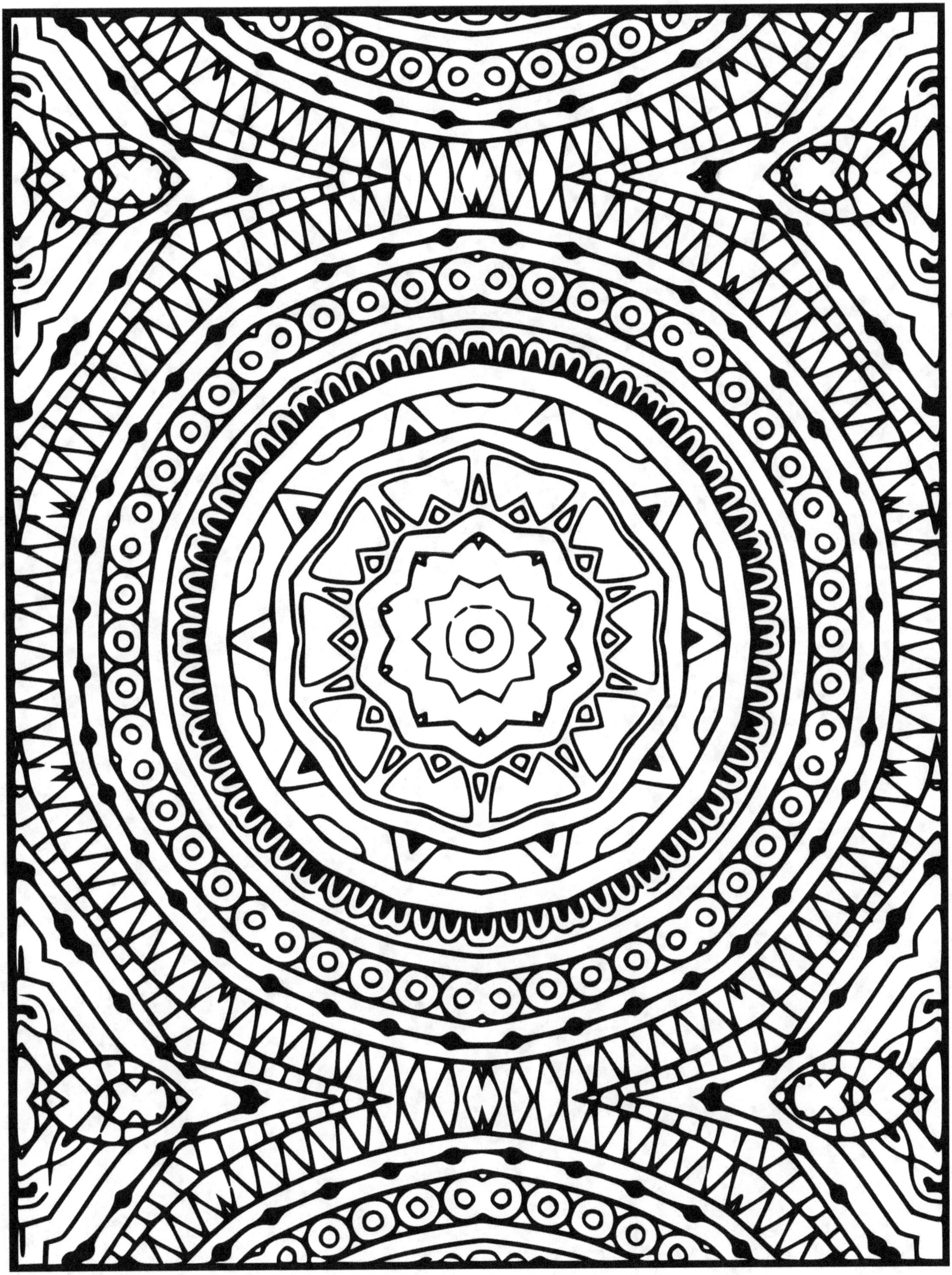

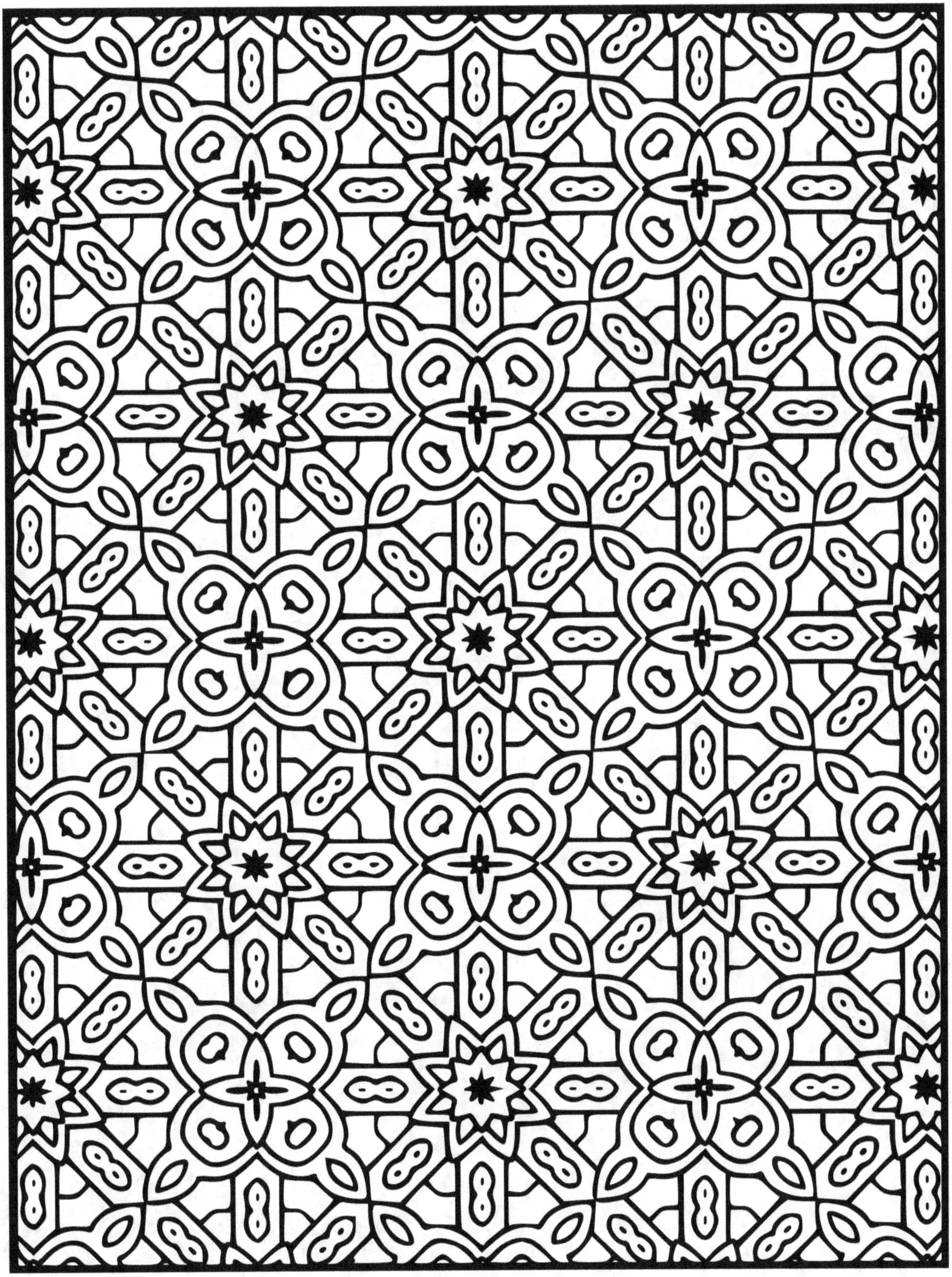

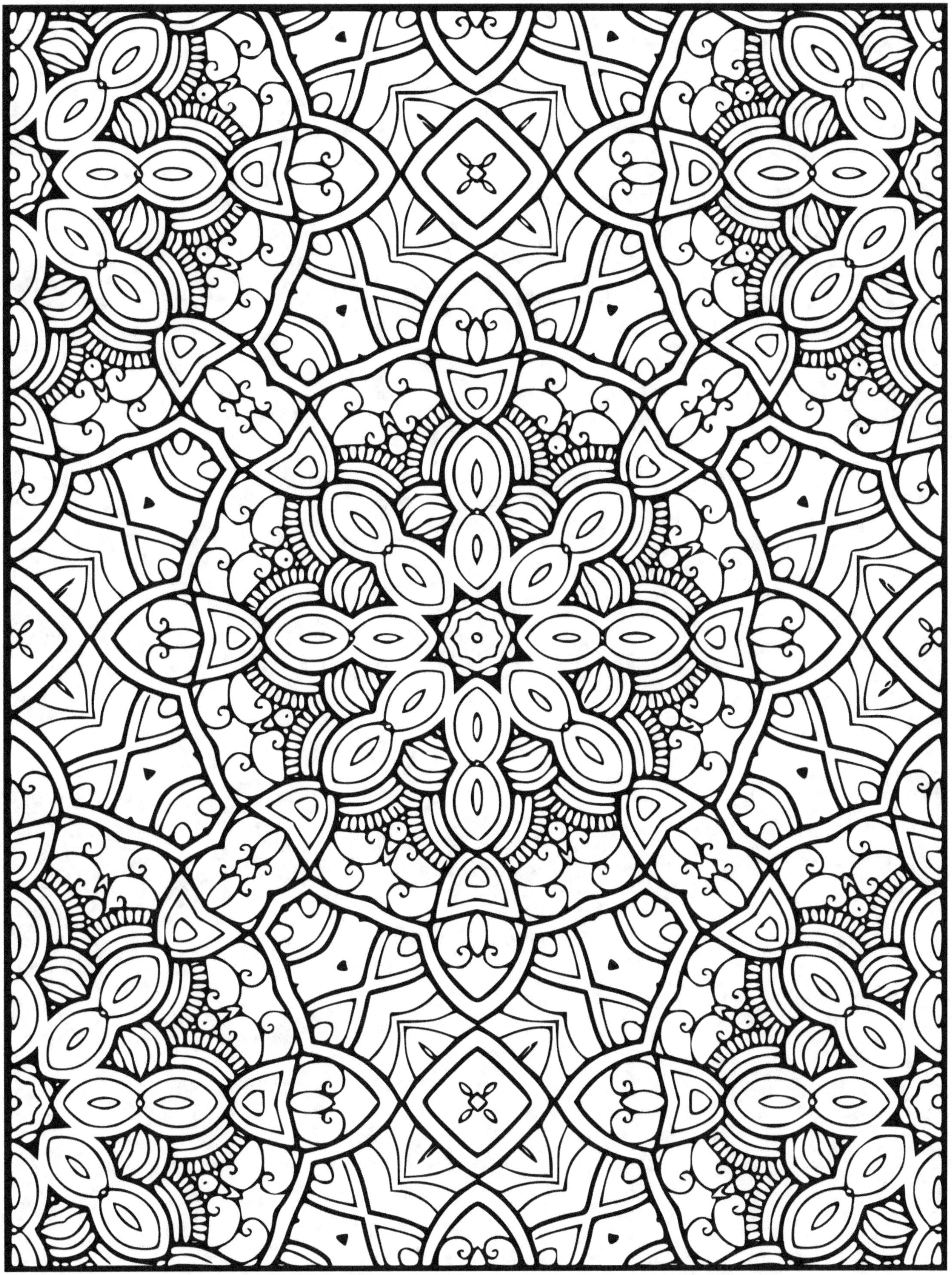

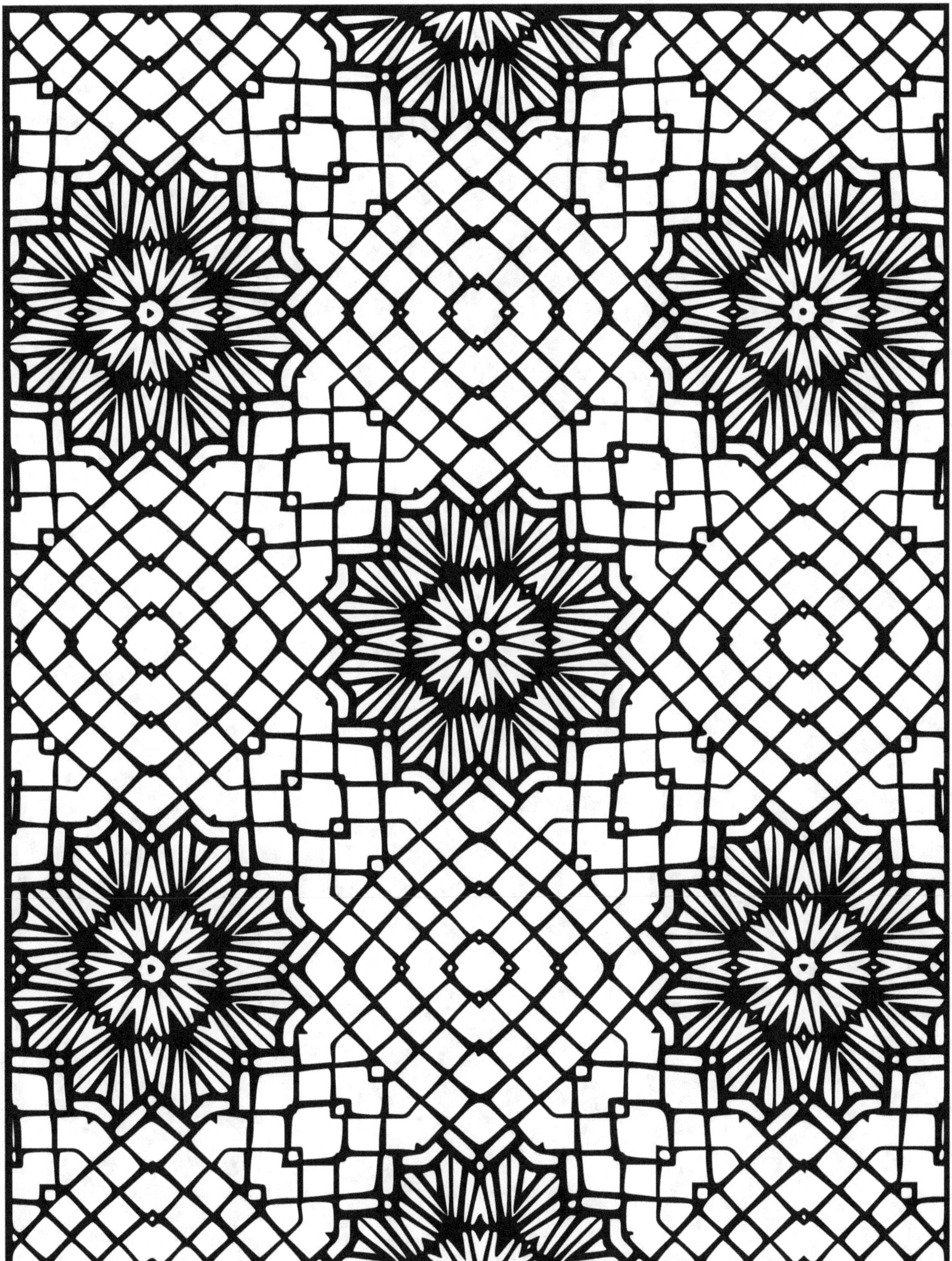

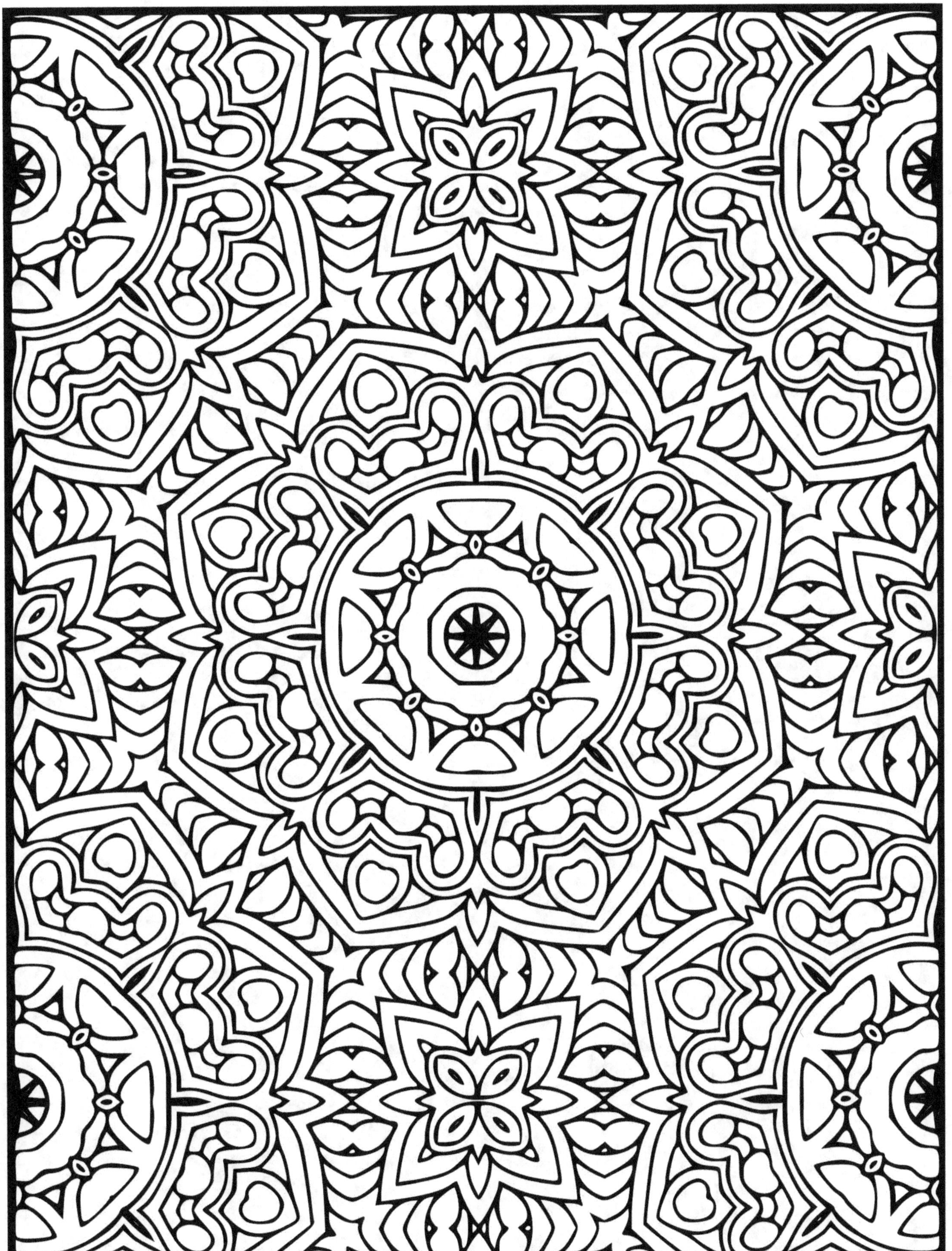

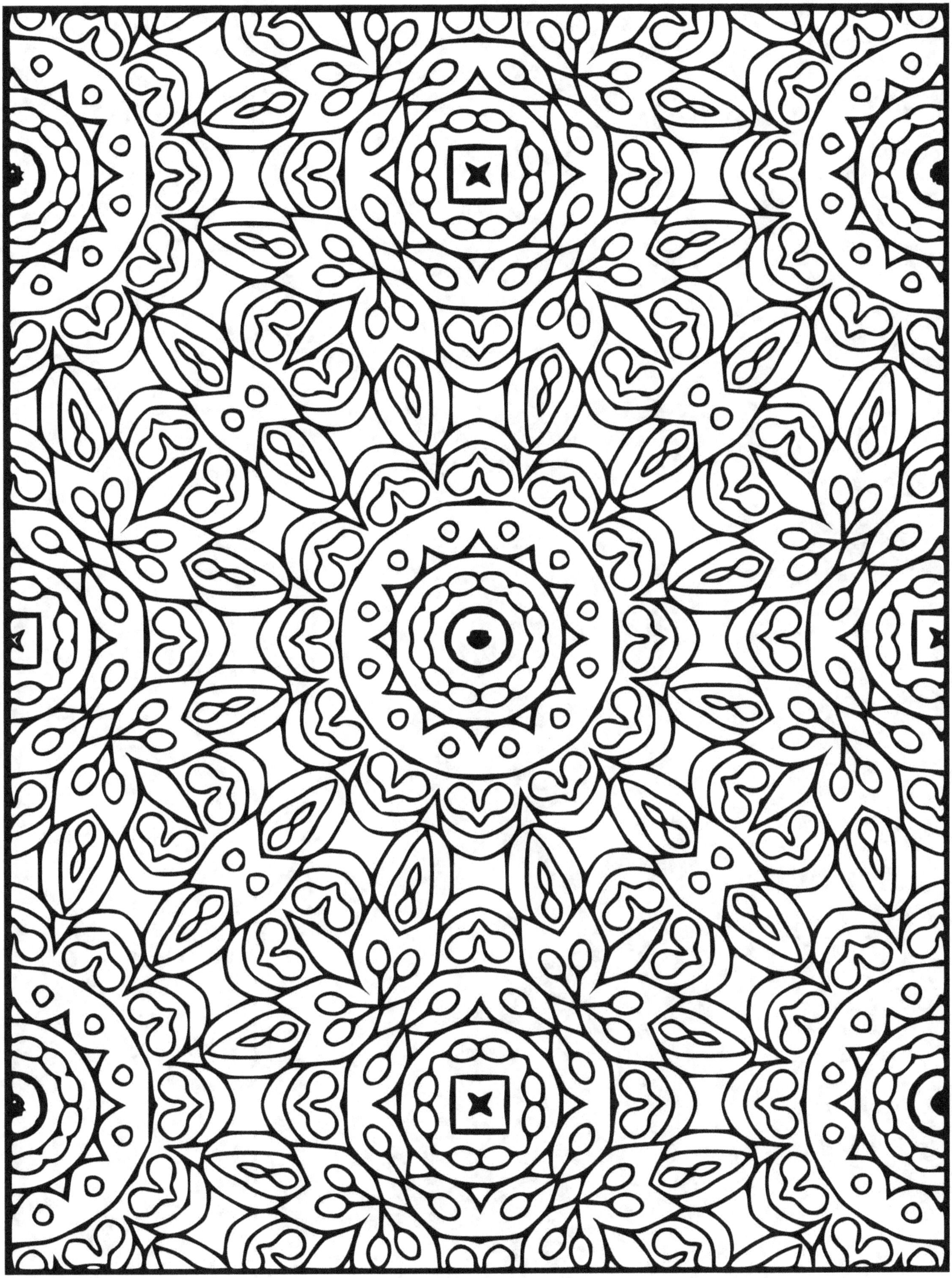

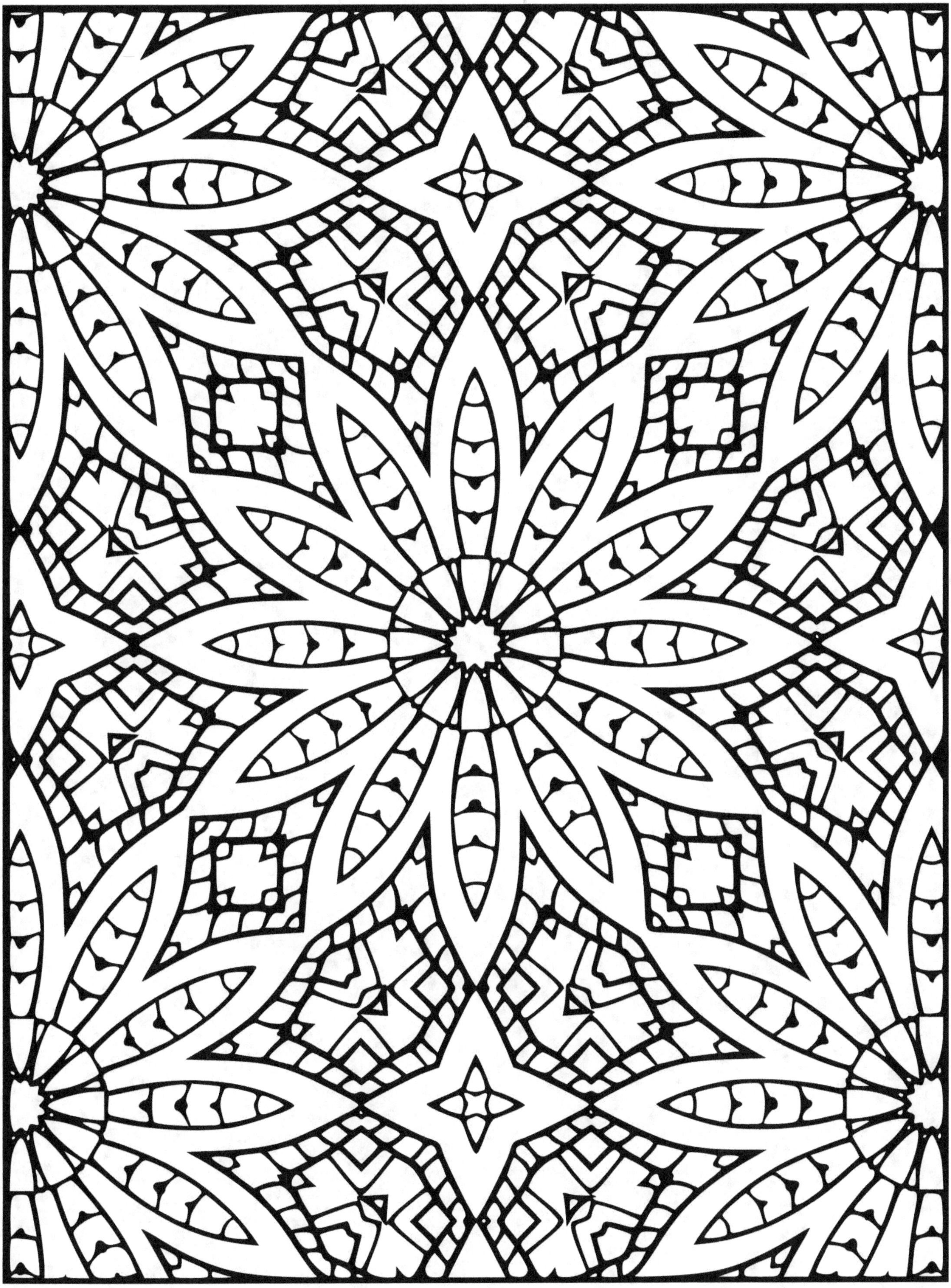

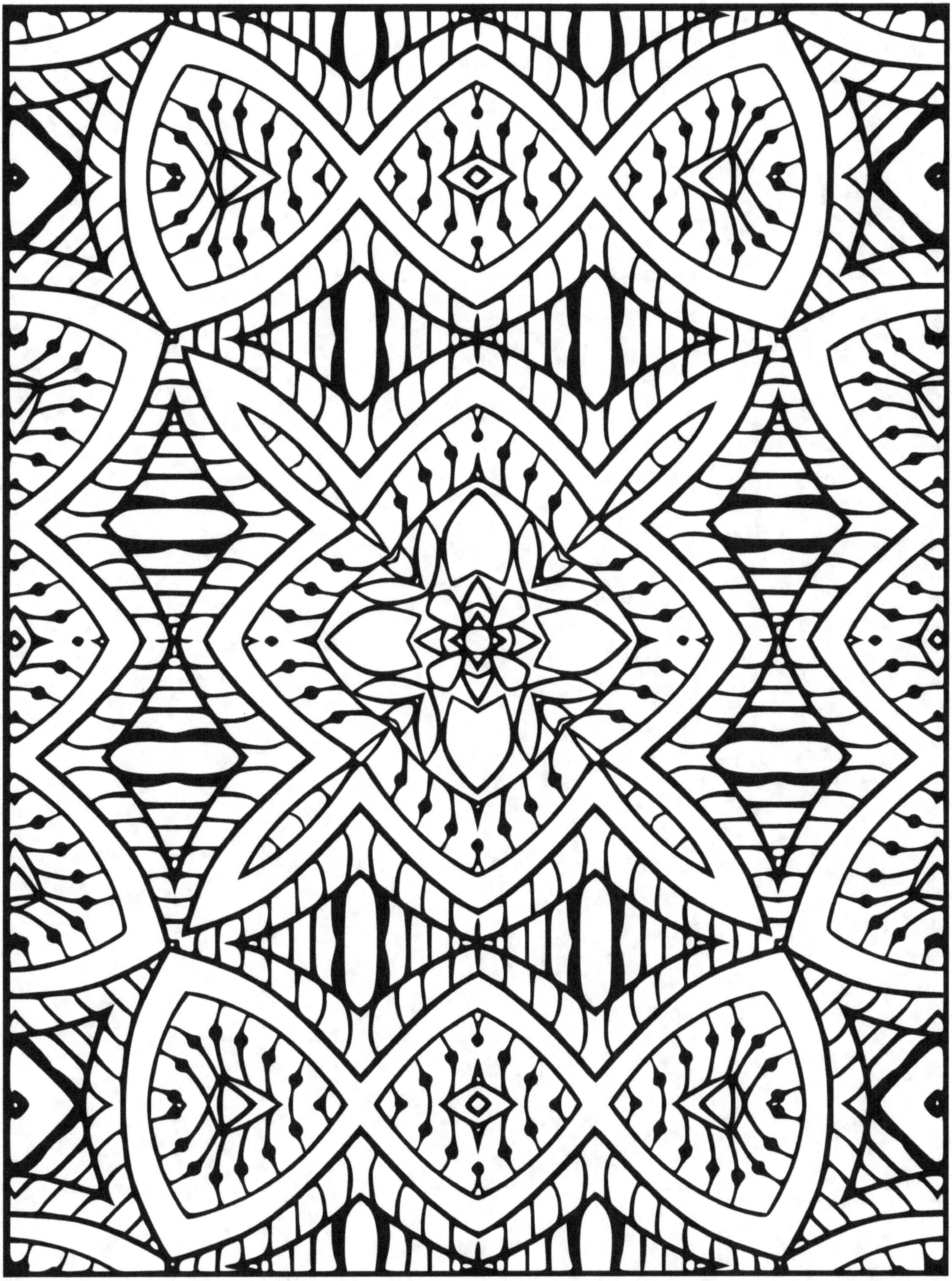

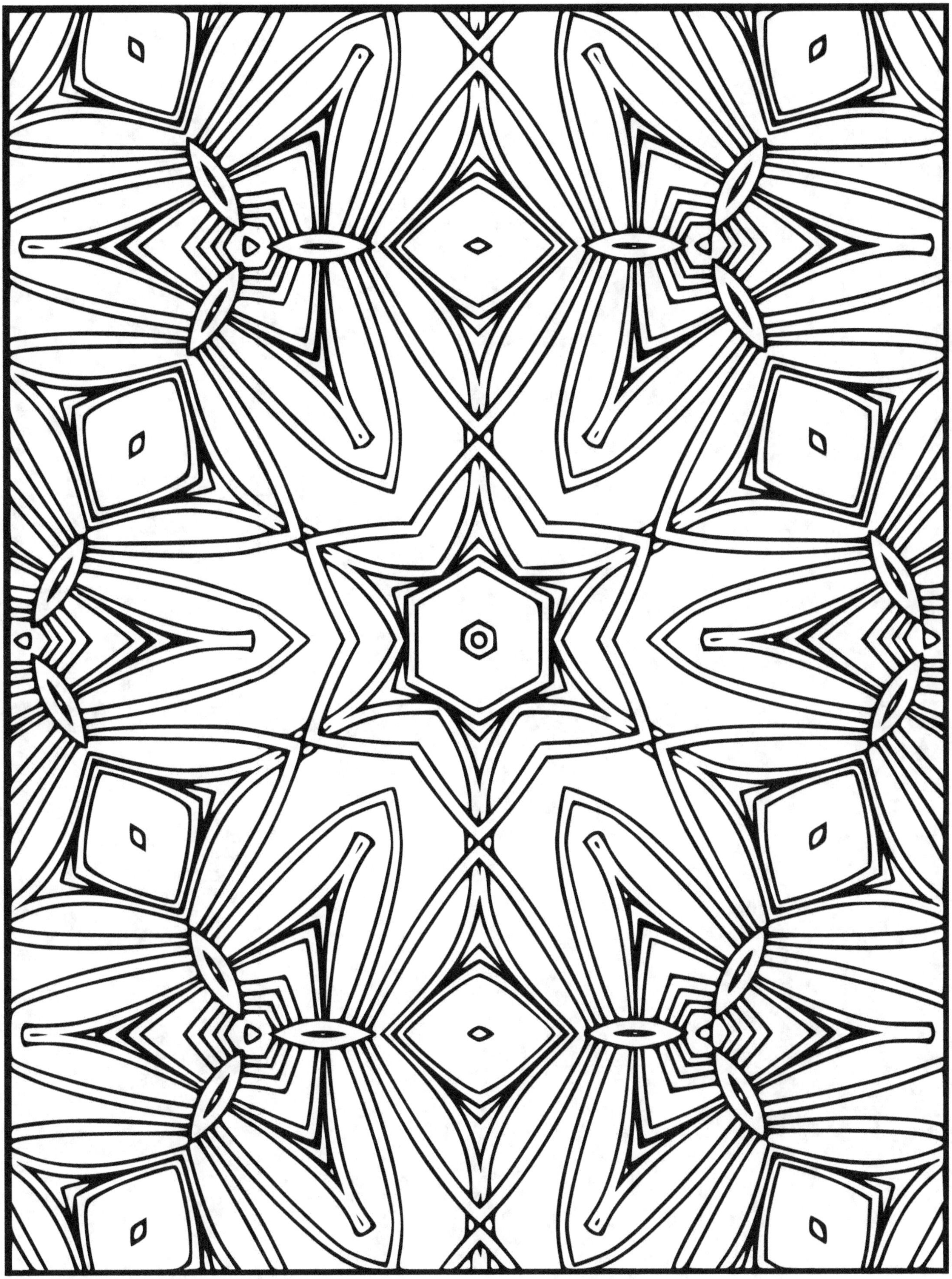

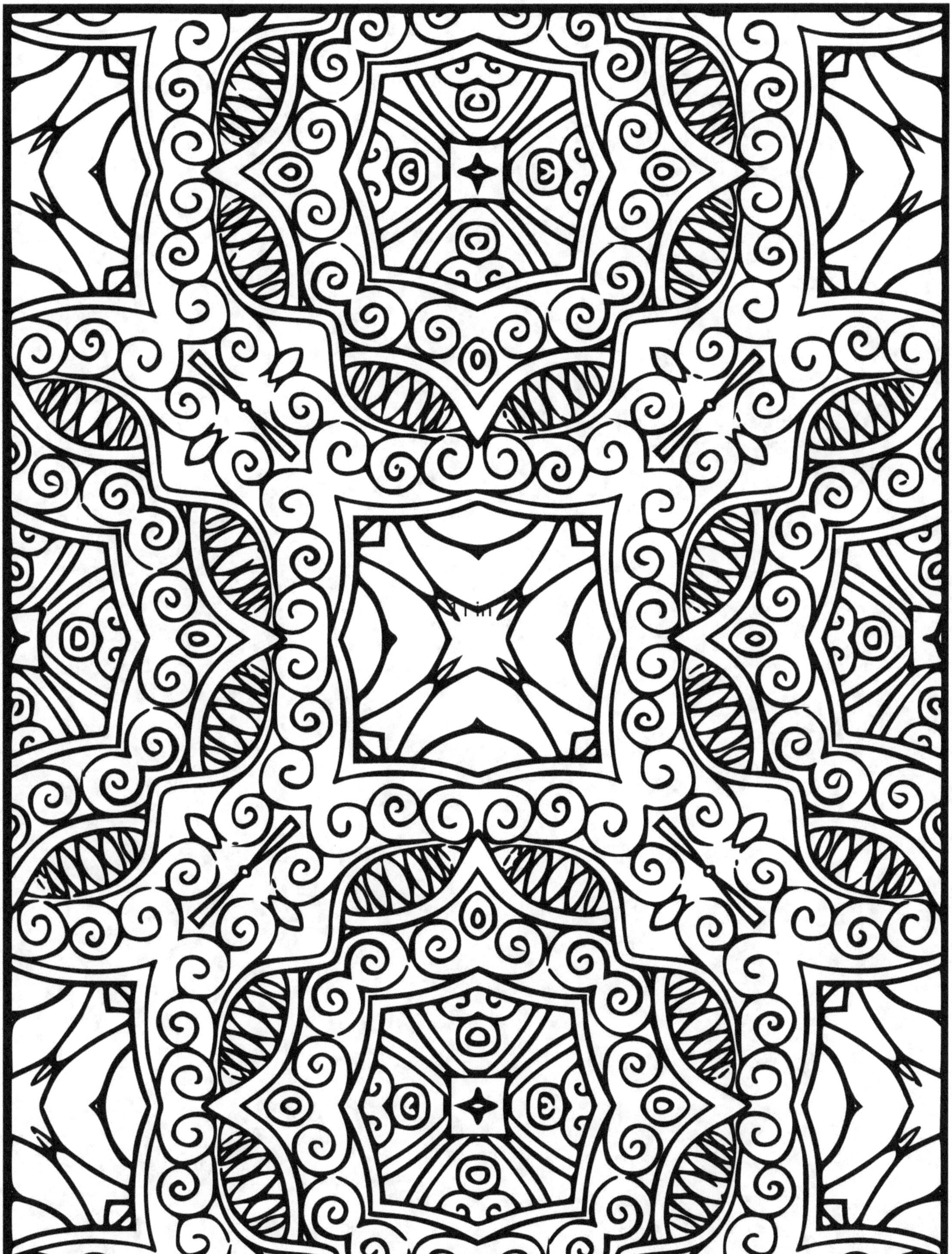

www.ingramcontent.com/pod-product-compliance
Lightning Source LLC
Chambersburg PA
CBHW081538220526
45467CB00010B/3249
* 9 7 9 8 6 9 3 0 9 2 5 2 5 *